NOT FOR CIRCULATION

JOAN OF ARC

WOMEN of ACHIEVEMENT

JOAN OF ARC

Dwayne E. Pickels

CHELSEA HOUSE PUBLISHERS
PHILADELPHIA

Frontispiece: This 16th century illustration from "Vie des femmes celebres" (Lives of Famous Women) depicts Jeanne d'Arc riding triumphantly in her customized armor and bearing the standard (banner).

Chelsea House Publishers
EDITOR IN CHIEF Sally Cheney
DIRECTOR OF PRODUCTION Kim Shinners
PRODUCTION MANAGER Pamela Loos
ART DIRECTOR Sara Davis
EDITOR Bill Conn
PRODUCTION EDITOR Diann Grasse
LAYOUT 21st Century Publishing and Communications, Inc.

The Chelsea House World Wide Web address is
http://www.chelseahouse.com

First Printing
1 3 5 7 9 8 6 4 2

Pickels, Dwayne E.
    Joan of Arc / Dwayne E. Pickels.
        p. cm. — (Women of achievement)
    Includes bibliographical references and index.
    Summary: A biography of the young French woman who, inspired by visions supposedly from God, led the French army against English invaders, was burned at the stake as a heretic, and eventually was declared a saint.
    ISBN 0-7910-6314-3 (alk. paper)
    1. Joan, of Arc, Saint, 1412-1431—Juvenile literature. 2. Christian women saints—France—Biography—Juvenile literature. 3. Hundred Years§'War, 1339–1453—Juvenile literature. 4. France—History—Charles VII, 1422–1461—Juvenile literature. [1. Joan, of Arc, Saint, 1412–1431. 2. Saints. 3. Women—Biography. 4. France—History—Charles VII, 1422–1461.] I. Title. II. Series.

DC103.5 .P53 2001
944'.026'092—dc21
[B]   2001047379

CONTENTS

WOMEN OF ACHIEVEMENT

Jane Addams
SOCIAL WORKER

Madeleine Albright
STATESWOMAN

Marian Anderson
SINGER

Susan B. Anthony
WOMAN SUFFRAGIST

Joan of Arc
FRENCH SAINT AND HEROINE

~~**Clara Barton**~~ *Rachel*
AMERICAN RED CROSS FOUNDER

Rachel ~~Carson~~ *Barton*
BIOLOGIST AND AUTHOR

Cher
SINGER AND ACTRESS

Cleopatra
QUEEN OF EGYPT

Hillary Rodham Clinton
FIRST LADY AND ATTORNEY

Katie Couric
JOURNALIST

Diana, Princess of Wales
HUMANITARIAN

Emily Dickinson
POET

Elizabeth Dole
POLITICIAN

Amelia Earhart
AVIATOR

Gloria Estefan
SINGER

Jodie Foster
ACTRESS AND DIRECTOR

Ruth Bader Ginsburg
SUPREME COURT JUSTICE

Katherine Graham
PUBLISHER

Helen Hayes
ACTRESS

Mahalia Jackson
GOSPEL SINGER

Helen Keller
HUMANITARIAN

Ann Landers/ Abigail Van Buren
COLUMNISTS

Barbara McClintock
BIOLOGIST

Margaret Mead
ANTHROPOLOGIST

Julia Morgan
ARCHITECT

Toni Morrison
AUTHOR

Grandma Moses
PAINTER

Lucretia Mott
WOMAN SUFFRAGIST

Sandra Day O'Connor
SUPREME COURT JUSTICE

Rosie O'Donnell
ENTERTAINER AND COMEDIAN

Georgia O'Keeffe
PAINTER

Eleanor Roosevelt
DIPLOMAT AND HUMANITARIAN

Wilma Rudolph
CHAMPION ATHLETE

Diane Sawyer
JOURNALIST

Elizabeth Cady Stanton
WOMAN SUFFRAGIST

Martha Stewart
ENTREPRENEUR

Harriet Beecher Stowe
AUTHOR AND ABOLITIONIST

Barbra Streisand
ENTERTAINER

Amy Tan
AUTHOR

Elizabeth Taylor
ACTRESS AND ACTIVIST

Mother Teresa
HUMANITARIAN AND RELIGIOUS LEADER

Barbara Walters
JOURNALIST

Edith Wharton
AUTHOR

Phillis Wheatley
POET

Oprah Winfrey
ENTERTAINER

"REMEMBER THE LADIES"

MATINA S. HORNER

"Remember the Ladies." That is what Abigail Adams wrote to her husband John, then a delegate to the Continental Congress, as the Founding Fathers met in Philadelphia to form a new nation in March of 1776. "Be more generous and favorable to them than your ancestors. Do not put such unlimited power in the hands of the Husbands. If particular care and attention is not paid to the Ladies," Abigail Adams warned, "we are determined to foment a Rebellion, and will not hold ourselves bound by any Laws in which we have no voice, or Representation."

The words of Abigail Adams, one of the earliest American advocates of women's rights, were prophetic. Because when we have not "remembered the ladies," they have, by their words and deeds, reminded us so forcefully of the omission that we cannot fail to remember them. For the history of American women is as interesting and varied as the history of our nation as a whole. American women have played an integral part in founding, settling, and building our country. Some we remember as remarkable women who—against great odds—achieved distinction in the public arena: Anne Hutchinson, who in the 17th century became a charismatic religious leader; Phillis Wheatley, an 18th-century black slave who became a poet; Susan B. Anthony, whose name is synonymous with the 19th-century women's rights movement, and who led the struggle to enfranchise women; and in the 20th century, Amelia Earhart, the first woman to cross the Atlantic Ocean by air.

These extraordinary women certainly merit our admiration, but other women, "common women," many of them all but forgotten, should also be recognized for their contributions to American thought and culture. Women have been community builders; they have founded schools and formed voluntary associations to help those in need; they have assumed the major responsibility for rearing children, passing on from one generation to the next the values that keep a culture alive. These and innumerable other contributions, once ignored, are now being recognized by scholars, students, and the public. It is exciting and gratifying that a part of our history that was hardly acknowledged a few generations ago is now being studied and brought to light.

In recent decades, the field of women's history has grown from obscurity to a politically controversial splinter movement to academic respectability, in many cases mainstreamed into such traditional disciplines as history, economics, and psychology. Scholars of women, both female and male, have organized research centers at such prestigious institutions as Wellesley College, Stanford University, and the University of California. Other notable centers for women's studies are the Center for the American Woman and Politics at the Eagleton Institute of Politics at Rutgers University; the Henry A. Murray Research Center for the Study of Lives, at Radcliffe College; and the Women's Research and Education Institute, the research arm of the Congressional Caucus on Women's Issues. Other scholars and public figures have established archives and libraries, such as the Schlesinger Library on the History of Women in America, at Radcliffe College, and the Sophia Smith Collection, at Smith College, to collect and preserve the written and tangible legacies of women.

From the initial donation of the Women's Rights Collection in 1943, the Schlesinger Library grew to encompass vast collections documenting the manifold accomplishments of American women. Simultaneously, the women's movement in general and the academic discipline of women's studies in particular also began with a narrow definition and gradually expanded their mandate. Early causes, such as woman suffrage and social reform, abolition, and organized labor were joined by newer concerns, such as the history of women in business and the professions and in politics and government; the study of the family; and social issues such as health policy and education.

Women, as historian Arthur M. Schlesinger, jr., once pointed out, "have constituted the most spectacular casualty of traditional history. They have made up at least half the human race, but you could never tell that by looking at the books historians write." The new breed of historians is remedying that omission. They have written books about immigrant women and about working-class women who struggled for survival in cities and about black women who met the challenges of life in rural areas. They are telling the stories of women who, despite the barriers of tradition and economics, became lawyers and doctors and public figures.

The women's studies movement has also led scholars to question traditional interpretations of their respective disciplines. For example, the study of war has traditionally been an exercise in military and political analysis, an examination of strategies planned and executed by men. But scholars of women's history have pointed out that wars have also been periods of tremendous change and even opportunity for women, because the very absence of men on the home front enabled them to expand their educational, economic, and professional activities and to assume leadership in their homes.

The early scholars of women's history showed a unique brand of courage in choosing to investigate new subjects and take new approaches to old ones. Often, like their subjects, they endured criticism and even ostracism by their academic colleagues. But their efforts have unquestionably been worthwhile, because with the publication of each new study and book another piece of the historical patchwork is sewn into place, revealing an increasingly comprehensive picture of the role of women in our rich and varied history.

Such books on groups of women are essential, but books that focus on the lives of individuals are equally indispensable. Biographies can be inspirational, offering their readers the example of people with vision who have looked outside themselves for their goals and have often struggled against great obstacles to achieve them. Marian Anderson, for instance, had to overcome racial bigotry in order to perfect her art and perform as a concert singer. Isadora Duncan defied the rules of classical dance to find true artistic freedom. Jane Addams had to break down society's notions of the proper role for women in order to create new social situations, notably the settlement house. All of these women had to come to terms both with themselves and with the world in which they lived. Only then could they move ahead as pioneers in their chosen callings.

Biography can inspire not only by adulation but also by realism. It helps us to see not only the qualities in others that we hope to emulate, but also, perhaps, the weaknesses that made them "human." By helping us identify with the subject on a more personal level they help us feel that we, too, can achieve such goals. We read about Eleanor Roosevelt, for instance, who occupied a unique and seemingly enviable position as the wife of the president. Yet we can sympathize with her inner dilemma; an inherently shy woman, she had to force herself to live a most public life in order to use her position to benefit others. We may not be able to imagine ourselves having the immense poetic talent of Emily Dickinson, but from her story we can understand the challenges faced by a creative woman who was expected to fulfill many family responsibilities. And though few of us will ever reach the level of athletic accomplishment displayed by Wilma Rudolph or Babe Zaharias, we can still appreciate their spirit, their overwhelming will to excel.

A biography is a multifaceted lens. It is first of all a magnification, the intimate examination of one particular life. But at the same time, it is a wide-angle lens, informing us about the world in which the subject lived. We come away from reading about one life knowing more about the social, political, and economic fabric of the time. It is for this reason, perhaps, that the great New England essayist Ralph Waldo Emerson wrote in 1841, "There is properly no history: only biography." And it is also why biography, and particularly women's biography, will continue to fascinate writers and readers alike.

This 15th century illustration depicts Jeanne being tied to the stake on the day of her execution May 30, 1431.

1

THE HERETIC OF THE HUNDRED YEARS' WAR

It is May 30, 1431. The fire is kindling beneath Joan's bare feet, and thin wisps of smoke rise toward her face. Soon, flames reach her skin and the heat becomes excruciatingly intense, transforming Joan's dread into stark agony. Before long the smoke obscures her view of the judges, captors, and tormentors. This 19-year-old French peasant girl has been unfairly labeled a heretic, blasphemer, and sorceress. But her only request while tied to a stake to be burned to death is to hold and gaze upon a crucifix and surrender her spirit to God.

In Joan's brief life she had managed extraordinary achievements: she had inspired her fellow countrymen, she had seen to it that her king was crowned, and she had set her nation back on the path to glory. Her religious convictions had seen her through the horrors of numerous bloody wars—Joan had even gone into battle herself for the sake of her king—and had kept her alive when she was betrayed by the man whom she'd helped to enthrone.

Yet, it was in her final moments on that day in May that an English soldier—a former sworn enemy—hurriedly fashioned a crude cross out of a broken stick. He handed it to the dying girl, who kissed it and prayed as she tucked it into the front of her robe. This was one of the few times in the past two years that Joan had not been dressed as a man—a habit that was viewed as one of the worst sins she could commit and one of the transgressions for which she was being put to death. While members of the crowd wept in pity and horror, Joan silently asked God to forgive her killers. She cried out six times in a sure, strong voice a single word: "Jesus."

Who was Joan of Arc, the young girl who had accomplished such great things? In her lifetime she was not known as Joan, which is the English version of her name, but as *Jeanne*. According to a statement made during her trial, the French maiden who would become an icon of Christian faith was born either in 1411 or 1412. In a June 1429 letter from Perceval de Boulainvilliers, a counselor to Charles VII, Jeanne's birth is described as having fallen on the Christian night of Epiphany (also called "Twelfth Night"). This feast is celebrated on January 6 by today's calendars.

Jeanne was a daughter of a peasant couple who lived in the tiny village of Domrémy. According to a contemporary account in the book *Dramatis Personae* by Pierre Champion, Jeanne's father, Jacques or Jacquot Darc, was born circa 1375 at Ceffonds, in the diocese of Troyes. "It was about the time of his marriage that he established himself at Domrémy," Champion writes. His wife, Isabelle Romée, came from the nearby village of Vouthon. Historians contend that Jacques held an honorable position in his region and may have been a man of some wealth. Champion reports that in 1419, Jacques Darc bought the Chateau de l'Ile at a local auction. In a 1423 document Jacques is described as a *doyen*, or sergeant, of the village. This a rank is somewhere between our present-day positions of mayor and provost. One of Jacques' duties was to collect taxes, and he was also one of seven notable men who was a

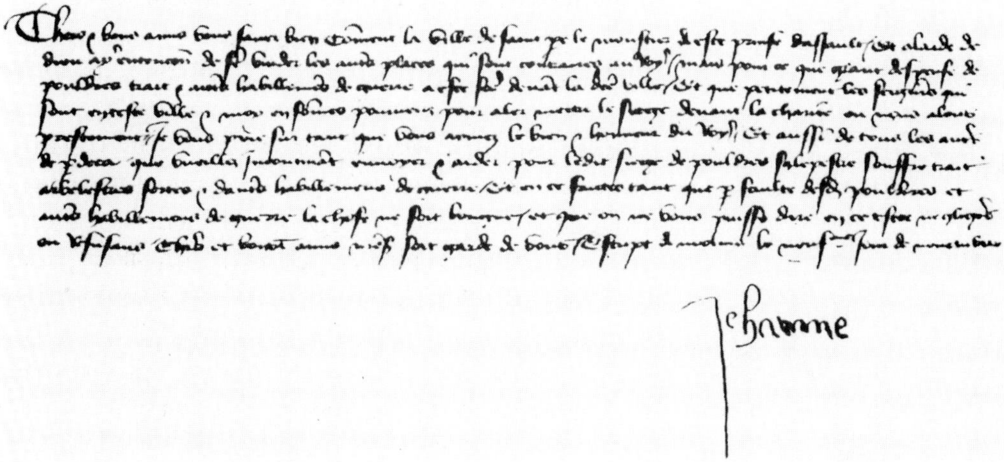

[handwritten letter in medieval French, signed "Jehanne"]

This is a letter composed by Jeanne d'Arc. It bears her signature. Handwriting experts believe her to be left-handed.

delegate for his village in legal matters. Other records show that in 1427 Jacques acted once again as a village delegate in an important trial held before Robert de Baudricourt, the captain of Vaucouleurs. Darc was made a noble in December 1429. Jeanne's mother, Isabelle (or Isabeau), was also called Romée—a name derived from a title given to her mother for having completed a pilgrimage to Rome. Isabelle was made a noble with her husband in 1429.

The couple's daughter Jeanne would come to be known by many names. During her military career she was called *Jeanne la Pucelle*—"Jeanne the Maiden." She was also known as "the Maid of Lorraine," or sometimes simply "the Maid." The nickname appears to have been a testament to her vow of chastity: Jeanne is said to have sworn at age 13 to maintain her virginity "for as long as it should please God." Lorraine was the name of the French territory where her village was located. The largely agricultural community of Domrémy rested along the Meuse River in northern France. Curiously, ancient legends had claimed that Lorraine would be the birthplace of a virgin who would one day save France.

In medieval manuscripts, Jeanne's surname appears

in numerous forms: Darc, Tarc, Tart, Dare, Day, Daix, and others. Yet another surname has been associated with the Darcs as well—"*du Lys*," which means "of the Lily." The Darcs received this name when Jacques was granted a patent of nobility by King Charles VII in 1429, while Jeanne herself was in battle on his behalf. Jeanne's brothers' surnames are listed as "Darc du Lys" in some documents of the period.

Jeanne herself rarely used the Darc surname. Instead, she frequently referred to herself simply as *la Pucelle* (the Maid). When Jeanne was asked during her final trial to give her surname, she replied that said she knew nothing of such a name. Later in the proceedings, she gave her surname as either Darc or Romée (young girls in her region frequently adopted their mother's surname).

Jeanne had three brothers, Jacques, Jean, and Pierre, and a sister, Catherine. Pierre followed Jeanne to "France"—which is the word Jeanne often used during her trial in place of French city names. He fought beside her at Orléans and lived in the same house with her there. Later he accompanied her to Reims and was ennobled with the rest of the family in 1429. He was also captured with Jeanne at Compiègne.

Sources disagree about the order in which Jacques and Isabelle Darc's brood was born, but we can be relatively certain that Jeanne was born around the time when the feudal conflict in France resumed. The country was firmly in the grip of what would become known as the Hundred Years' War, which began in 1337 when feudal quarrels re-ignited old rivalries traced back to 1066. That was the year that William the Conqueror, the French duke from Normandy, invaded and won the throne of England.

Intermittent fighting between France and England had been suspended in 1396 by a truce; still, battles continually broke out. "The major war was not a cataclysmic horror," writes *Joan of Arc* author Mary Gordon, "but the drawn-out dance of nearly a century of fruitless

and debilitating destruction. Rather than imagining a great blaze, we should think of a series of small brushfires that are never put out but smolder continually, creating a noxious smoke and sparking other small fires in the vicinity, filling the air with poisonous vapors and destroying the land's possibilities for productive habitation."

In 1411, an open civil war broke out in Jeanne's homeland. The conflict was among several French nobles, which fell into two factions—the Burgundians and the Armagnacs. Both groups had sought aid from various nobles in England, but when the English King Henry V invaded Normandy, the war between the countries was once again in play. Around the same time, France was

This engraving depicts the Battle of Agincourt (1415) in which the English under Henry V reconquered Normandy. The Dauphin was forced to flee to the South of France and the Burgundians took over the reigns of power. This was the political stage onto which young Jeanne was thrust.

struggling to recover from a deadly outbreak of bubonic plague (sometimes called the "Black Death"), which decimated half of France's entire population.

Despite ever-present reminders of war and pestilence, it appears that Jeanne had a relatively normal and happy childhood in Domrémy. She frolicked and played with her friends in the fields, and she worked beside her parents and siblings at home, a modest building by today's standards. Although it's difficult to imagine that such a building could have survived nearly 600 years, many history books include a photograph of a two-story stone home with a steeply slanted roof that still stands in the village of Domrémy and is believed to have been Jeanne's birthplace. The land around the home probably had a garden and was most likely connected to a stable, in which cattle and sheep were housed.

Historians surmise that the house had a clay floor, where Jeanne probably spent time sitting by the hearth in the evenings. Like other young girls in the village, she learned to spin wool and was taught to do most household chores. From her devout mother, Jeanne learned the most common Catholic prayers, including the *Pater Noster* ("Our Father"), *Ave Maria* ("Hail Mary"), and the *Credo* (the Creed, a prayer that briefly outlines the basic beliefs of Catholics). In Albert Bigelow Paine's book, *The Girl in the White Armor: The True Story of Joan of Arc*, Jeanne is described by a child-hood friend Mangette as "good, simple, and sweet." Paine also portrays young Jeanne as having great concern for the poor: she often gave up her bed to those whom her parents took in and slept on the floor by the hearth. Other sources report that even as a child she frequently gave alms to the poor (the money would come from her father).

Like her mother, Jeanne appears to have been a devout Catholic from a very young age: she attended church often and was sometimes teased by others for her devotion. She received the sacrament of confession

The humble home in which Jeanne spent her childhood. She was born in this home in 1412 and left home at the age of 16 to Vaucouleurs in 1428 to follow her spiritual and military mission.

regularly as well. In those times, most people had a "confessor," a priest to whom they regularly confessed their sins. According to Frances Gies, in *Joan of Arc: The Legend and the Reality,* Jeanne's confessor, Guillaume Front, who was the curate of the church in Domrémy, was struck by Jeanne's exceptional piety. Front, according to Gies, "had been heard to say that there was no one like [Jeanne] in the village and no better Catholic in his parish."

Jeanne did not know it, but the serenity of her childhood in Domrémy would not last. Before long, the young girl's life would be shaken to the core by God himself.

In this original painting by Thirion, Jeanne hears the "voices" from heaven.

2

VOICES

Many historians agree that Jeanne was 12 or 13 years old when she first began to hear "voices" that she claimed were God's saints speaking to her. Others say she was somewhat older when these voices began calling Jeanne into service. It's difficult to know when Jeanne's "messages" began to come to her, and it is impossible to know whether they were elements of her imagination or whether they were authentic. Whatever the truth was, most historians agree that Jeanne truly believed that she was hearing messages from God. At first Jeanne believed that the messages were being delivered by "angels"; later she would say that the messengers were Saints Michael, Catherine, and Margaret.

We may view Jeanne's claim of hearing messages from God as far-fetched today, but in her time many believed that such visitations from messengers of God were not only possible, but highly probable. People believed that the devil was equally capable of sending messages to earth—and to be less than certain of one's faith could result in a misplaced trust in evil and a fall from grace, or from God's protection.

Jeanne believed that she knew exactly where her voices came from. At first, they simply told her to "be a good girl and go to church often," and she was happy to obey. No doubt it was comforting for her to do so. Travelers passing through Domrémy often brought news of war and disease in the "outside" world to the elders of the village, and Jeanne and her young friends likely listened in fear and amazement.

Domrémy had so far been spared most of the turmoil, thanks in large part to the local lord, Robert de Baudricourt, who resided in nearby Vaucouleurs. De Baudricourt was loyal to the Armagnacs, who supported the dauphin Charles's right to the French crown. (The king's eldest son is called the *dauphin* or heir to the throne.) However, Domrémy was closer to Burgundy than to the walled city of Vaucouleurs, and thus Vaucouleurs would ultimately offer little protection to Domrémy from raids against the Armagnacs. As a result, the residents of Domrémy rented an abandoned fortress on a nearby island in the Meuse River. They planned to send the women, children, and animals of the village to this fortress in the event of attack, whether from the English or from the Burgundians. Unfortunately, too soon they would be forced to make use of the haven. When Jeanne was not yet a teenager, a party of Burgundian soldiers pressing toward Vaucouleurs set upon Domrémy and burned the defenseless village to the ground.

This destruction happened around the same time that Jeanne began hearing her voices. During her trial, she would explain that St. Catherine and St. Margaret informed her to seek Robert de Baudricourt's aid in receiving passage to Chinon, where dauphin Charles resided. There, she needed an audience with Charles. The obstacles were enormous for a trained soldier, but seemingly impossible—and extremely unusual—for an uneducated peasant girl. Jeanne needed to convince the lord somehow that her mission was legitimate. If she succeeded, she would have to travel through more than 300 miles of predominantly Burgundian territory, a perilous journey that historians estimate would have taken 10 to 13 days. If she arrived in Chinon without being captured or killed, she still had to convince the heir to the throne, who made scarcely a move without the counsel of his ministers, to give her an army with which to battle the English. It was an unprecedented mission. The young girl from Domrémy, however, believed she had no choice.

It was May 1428. The English, along with some Burgundians had launched a siege on the city of Orléans, a strategically important city to the west of Domrémy. If the city were to fall, England would take all of France; it already held the capital city of Paris. Amid these circumstances, Jeanne Darc, almost 17 years old, appeared before the captain at Vaucouleurs and made the following plea:

> I have come to you on the part of my Lord in order that you may send word to the Dauphin to hold fast and not to cease the war against his enemies. Before mid-Lent the Lord will give him help. In truth, the kingdom belongs not to the Dauphin but to my Lord. But my Lord wills that the Dauphin be made King, and have the kingdom in command. Notwithstanding his enemies, the Dauphin will be made King, and it is I who will conduct him to the coronation.

An astonished de Baudricourt asked, "Who is your lord?" Jeanne replied: "The King of Heaven." His initial response to this incredible request was to order the girl returned to her father "for a sound thrashing." Still, Jeanne was persistent. She cited several prophecies that proclaimed that France "would be ruined through a woman, and afterward restored by a virgin," according to the historian Gies. The "woman" was said at the time to have been Queen Isabeau, the mother of Charles the Dauphin. Historians say that Isabeau of

Bavaria was loyal to both the Burgundians and the English and that she dashed Charles's chances to gain the throne by declaring him "illegitimate." She was not loyal to her husband, King Charles VI and was quite irresponsible with money.

Another contemporary prophecy, Gies writes, was believed to have originated from a mystic named Marie Robine, or Marie of Avignon. She foretold, "a Maid who would come after her would wear [armor] and deliver the kingdom of France from its enemies." Perhaps the most popular prophecy was attributed to the legendary Merlin of King Arthur's Court. Merlin is said to have predicted that "from the oak forest in the marches of Lorraine a virgin would come who would perform marvelous acts and save France." Nevertheless, Jeanne decided to return home to Domrémy.

In January 1429, Jeanne traveled for the second time to Vaucouleurs to deliver her message to Robert de Baudricourt. To Jean de Metz, one of the knights stationed there, she declared: "I must go, and I must do this, because my Lord wants me to do it." De Baudricourt once again refused to send her to Chinon. But Jeanne would not give up. A month later she went to him a third time. Finally, de Baudricourt reluctantly agreed to send the girl with an armed escort to see the dauphin.

Some reports say that de Baudricourt himself escorted "the Maid" to see Charles at Chinon. It is highly unlikely, however, that he did any more than agree to send her and provide an escort. According to Paine, de Baudricourt was "willing enough to be rid of" the persistent and odd young girl. Moreover, funding for the journey came not from de Baudricourt, but from citizens of Domrémy. It included second-hand clothing and a horse donated by Jeanne's uncle, Durand Laxart.

A party of seven set out for Chinon, led by de Metz, who is said to have been the first to believe Jeanne's story of the voices and of her mission from God.

ENGLISH CHANNEL

Calais
Agincourt
Arras
Cherbourg
Formigny
Harfleur
Dieppe
Somme
Compiègne
Rouen
Oise
Reims
Seine
Marne
Caen
Pontoise
Meaux
Falaise
Paris
Domrémy
NORMANDY
Mont-St-Michel
Vermeuil
Troyes
MAINE
Patay
Montereau
ANJOU
Orléans
Brest
BRITTANY
Jargeau
Dijon
Loire
Tours
DUCHY OF
BURGUNDY
Bourges
Saône
BERRY
POITOU
BOURBON
Dordogne
Rhône
Castillon
Bordeaux
Lot
Avignon
ALBRET
Garonne
Bayonne
ARMAGNAC
LANGUEDOC
Adour

Maximum extent of English influence

Burgundy (in France)

France (loyal to Charles, the dauphin)

Map showing France in 1429. At that time, most of France's land mass was under the power of the Dauphin. However, the capital city of Paris, as well as Normandy were ruled by the English. The little Duchy of Burgundy remained independent of both the Dauphin and the King of England.

Bertrand de Poulengy, a squire who had been in Robert's service, accompanied them, along with two messengers and two servants. Jeanne was clad in a pageboy's clothing, her hair cropped short as a boy's and a sword hanging from her belt. Later at her trial, she stated that she had been warned by the voices to don the garments of a man—actions that seemed scandalous and irreverent to many. It was a practical move, however: a young woman traveling through such hostile territory would only have invited more danger on the already perilous trip.

The small entourage traveled mostly at night, during the chilly winds of late winter. Because Burgundians and English soldiers were posted along many of the main roads, they were often forced to leave the well-established paths and forge their own way. Yet Jeanne said: "I do not fear the soldiers, for my road is made open to me; and if the soldiers come I have God, my Lord, who will know how to clear the route that leads to the Dauphin. It is for this that I was born."

Who was Charles the Dauphin, the man whom Jeanne fought so desperately to see and who would later become Charles VII, King of France? He has been described as weak-minded and weak-willed, disloyal, and treacherous. Other accounts paint a different picture of the man. In Regine Pernoud and Marie-Veronique Clin's *Joan of Arc: Her Story*, Charles is described by his contemporaries as "the Victorious" and as "sweet-tempered, gracious, full of piety and mercy, a fine person, of fine carriage and understanding." We know for certain that Jeanne herself believed in the latter characterization. "Speak not of my king; he is a good Christian," she reportedly told her accusers during her trial.

Born on February 22, 1403, Charles was the eleventh child and the fifth son of Charles VI and Isabeau. He outlived all his siblings and died at 58 on July 22, 1461. Charles was just 26 years old and his court in a shambles on the day when the young peasant girl from Lorraine came calling, claiming to have a mission from God to see him crowned king. Surrounded by a treacherous lot of advisors and counselors and facing a shrinking financial base, Charles had begun to use disreputable methods of obtaining new funds. He borrowed from loyal supporters, for example, and banished them from court to avoid repayment. Having lost Paris and now struggling with the besieged city of Orléans, his troops were utterly demoralized. The situation among the military was so bad that it was commonly said that 200 English soldiers "could put to flight 1,000 of the French."

If Jeanne thought that convincing Robert de Baudricourt to send her to Chinon was a difficult chore, she had yet to face the corruption and deceit of the dauphin's court. But she doesn't seem to have shown any hesitation. Jeanne's only recorded comment about her arrival in Chinon was that she "arrived near the King without interference and lodged first at an inn kept by an honest woman."

Word of the young maid of Lorraine's mission had preceded her. Her determination had already convinced a growing number of commoners that she was somehow a divinely chosen instrument of God. It is doubtful that Charles even received Jeanne's initial correspondences. Most likely they were intercepted and discarded by those who wished to control the indecisive heir to the throne. Eventually, however, even Charles himself heard tales of the young girl's fervent attempts to gain an audience with him. His advisors strongly warned him against seeing her: some had already begun to dub her a witch or a sorceress, and others thought she might be an assassin sent by the Burgundians or the English. Charles ignored their advice—and perhaps at the urging of others who saw in Jeanne's mission an opportunity for gain—ordered the girl brought before him.

A legend surrounds the first meeting between Jeanne Darc and Charles the Dauphin. As the tale goes, Charles decided to set someone up as himself while he stood anonymously in the court amid 300 other people. If God indeed sent Jeanne to see him, the reasoning was, she would surely spot the deception immediately and locate the true heir to the throne. Jeanne apparently did exactly that. Accounts say that she found the dauphin "retired behind some others" and immediately fell to his feet in reverence. Later, she would say only that she "recognized him by the counsel and revelation of my Voice." Some historians

Charles VII, King of France, who owed his ascent to the throne to a lowly peasant maiden. There are conflicting reports as to the true character of the Dauphin. Was he weak or morally upstanding? Regardless of the true nature of his character, Jeanne remained a faithful subject by her King throughout her trial.

claim that the tale is merely "embroidery" that has been added to the story of Jeanne's actual meeting with Charles. It is unlikely that Jeanne had ever seen Charles until that day, and while it's possible that she may have known him by the guidance of her "voices," several authors believe that Charles never played such a trick. Nevertheless, in later centuries several writers, including William Shakespeare, Mark Twain, and George Bernard Shaw, include it in their stories of Joan of Arc.

"Gentle Dauphin," Jeanne supposedly said, "my name is Jeanne, the Maid. The King of Heaven has sent me to bring you and your kingdom help." The court and the dauphin were astonished. Jeanne was led away to a private area, where she said, "Noble King, I am called Jeanne the Maid and I tell thee of the part of

Messire [God] that thou art the true inheritor of France, son of the King, and He sends me to conduct thee to Reims in order that thou receivest there thy coronation and thy sacrament, if such be thy wish."

How could he be certain she was sent from God, Charles asked Jeanne. Again, legend has it that she revealed her knowledge of a carefully guarded secret that she could not have known about through any other means. Some historians theorize that Jeanne told him he was not illegitimate, as Isabeau had labeled him. According to Paine, however, the king reported just before his death that Jeanne had recited verbatim a secret prayer he had uttered shortly before she had arrived in Chinon—a prayer that could have been known only to himself and to God.

Then Jeanne told Charles something even more astounding. This teenaged peasant girl who did not read or write, and who did not know how to wield the borrowed sword attached to her belt, informed the dauphin of France that she was prepared to go to war against the English and to lift the siege at Orléans.

For Jeanne to convince Charles that she had been sent by "the King of Heaven" was one thing; to convince him and his advisors that she should be given a full assembly of troops to save the besieged gateway to southern France was quite another. It was *impossible* that she was asking for control of the forces at Orléans. Only that city lay between victory and occupation by England. The dauphin had even begun entertaining plans of avoiding certain death or imprisonment by escaping to Scotland if the English troops were victorious. But the citizens of Orléans were desperate for relief from the daily assaults of fire and stone. They were running out of food and supplies—and hope.

Charles did not dismiss Jeanne out of hand, as one might expect. Rather, he ordered that she be examined by the learned men of the Church at Poitiers. Jeanne acceded to the dauphin's demands, but she grew impatient with the questions asked of her. "Why did God himself need soldiers," they asked her. Jeanne snapped: "In the name of God! The soldiers will fight and God will give the victory! In the name of God! I have not come to Poitiers to give signs, but take me to Orléans and I shall show you signs for which I have been sent!" They wanted to know what language her voices spoke. "They speak better French than you," she tartly replied.

Jeanne could not understand why they questioned her as though she had created the story herself. It was God's will that she was there, she told them repeatedly.

Remarkably, the priests of Poitiers confirmed Jeanne's story and advised Charles to accept her aid and to provide her with troops. Despite her impatience, a report from the examiners describes the young girl as filled with "humility, purity, devotion, and honesty." It is said, however, that Charles did not even wait for the report. Instead, he sent orders to raise a military force of which Jeanne would be *chef de guerre* (chief of war). He decreed that all captains and soldiers of all ranks at Orléans should heed her commands.

Two of the men who became part of Jeanne's forces were especially dear to Jeanne—they were her brothers, Jean and Pierre, who brought news that their mother had organized a pilgrimage to pray for her fearless daughter's success. Charles ordered a special suit of white armor fashioned for Jeanne. It cost 100 francs to create—a hefty sum that would have purchased eight war horses. But when Jeanne was clad in her armor atop her steed, she took on an "unearthly look."

What we know about the appearance of Joan of Arc's battle armor is based on a relief carving at the Abbey of St. Denis in France, where she left the suit after being ordered to pull out of Paris in 1429 (the location of the suit itself is unknown). With a tapered waist, wide hips, and an ornately engraved floral pattern, the armor has a feminine appearance and would not have fit the figure of a man. Its rigid plate metal must have been precisely tailored for Jeanne's body. It is also believed that the armor was not very thick or heavy. This is no doubt based on reports that Jeanne often wore her armor for days at a time, which would have been difficult with a thicker suit. And because a commander such as Jeanne was not expected to engage in battle herself, she was probably given lighter armor than a foot soldier would have worn.

Based on the St. Denis carving, scholars have learned about Jeanne's size. She is believed to have been about 4 feet, 8 inches—very petite by today's standards. But what was the Maid like? A counselor to Charles said that Jeanne "enjoys fine horses and arms, likes the company of noble knights, hates large gatherings and meetings, weeps readily, wears a cheerful countenance, and is incredibly strong in the wearing of armor and bearing of arms." Frances Gies writes that Perceval de Boulainvilliers, who had seen Jeanne himself, described the girl in a letter to Filippo Maria Visconti. Jeanne, said de Boulainvilliers, was "rather elegant; she bears herself vigorously, speaks little, shows an admirable prudence in her words. She has a feminine voice, eats little, drinks little wine."

Despite the grand armor, Jeanne still bore the nondescript sword given to her by Robert de Baudricourt. But her heavenly counselors instructed her to send for a special weapon buried near the altar of St. Catherine at Fierbois—the site of Jeanne's last stop before she had reached Chinon. Jeanne dispatched a messenger to the clergy at Fierbois with instructions for finding the sword. They discovered a rusting weapon marked with five crosses buried in shallow earth, just where she had said it would be. The majestic weapon was said to have once belonged to Charles Martel, a knight who offered it in sacrifice to St. Catherine after a victory over the Saracens in 732 A.D. Legend has it that the corrosion vanished at the first touch by the priests.

This engraving depicts the moment in which Jeanne received the sword of St. Catherine. She received communication from her "voices" as to the specific location of the buried sword. Originally, Charles Martel, the French crusader, owned the sword and offered it to St. Catherine in thanksgiving of victory over the Saracens in 732.

Jeanne was also given a standard—a special banner that she would raise high when she went into battle. Even more than the sword from St. Catherine, Jeanne cherished her standard. During her trial just two years later, Jeanne described her standard in loving detail. "I had a banner of which the field was strewn with lilies," she said. "The world was painted there, with two angels at the sides; it was white of the cloth called boucassin [a type of linen]; there was written on it, I believe, 'Jesus Maria' [Jesus and Mary]; it was fringed with silk." She loved her banner "better, forty times better" than her sword, she said, and instead of a weapon she carried the banner into battle.

Jeanne was apparently a skilled horsewoman, able to tame horses "so ill-tempered that no one would dare to ride them." Some accounts describe her entering Orléans on a white steed, one of the many animals given to her in admiration for her riding skills. Other sources report that she often rode black chargers into battle. One tale describes a new horse that was so resistant to being mounted by Jeanne that it refused to stand still. Jeanne, who was in the town of Selles at the time, instructed her knights to take the horse to the north door of the town church, where an old iron cross was affixed. When they did, the animal immediately calmed itself and allowed her to climb up "as though he were tied." Jeanne also is said to have predicted that she would be wounded during the siege of Orléans. "My blood will flow," she declared.

With all the grand legends surrounding Joan of Arc, it is important to remember that she was still a mere girl, a peasant from the tiny village of Domrémy, embarking on a mission for which nothing in her life could have prepared her. Amid the whirlwind of a royal court, surrounded by finery, she stood armed and shoulder to shoulder with brave men who were dedicated to fighting for their king and for the glory of France. Whether they believed she had been sent by God or not, these seasoned soldiers were about to follow a 17-year-old peasant girl into one of the fiercest battles of their lives.

Jeanne was morally opposed to the presence of camp followers (prostitutes who followed and were supported by the army). She desired an army composed of men who behaved as Christian gentlemen. In this 15th century manuscript, she is pictured violently casting out the camp followers.

3

THE SIEGE AT ORLÉANS

When Jeanne set out to lift the siege at Orléans in April 1429, she rode at the front of a column of 4,000 men, author Mary Gordon tells us. With her horsemen and men-at-arms were 400 head of cattle intended to feed the citizens of the besieged city and a squad of priests charged with maintaining the spiritual state of the troops. Gordon states that Jeanne insisted that the men confess their sins and receive Holy Communion. She also lectured them on reforming their coarse language.

One more condition Jeanne imposed on the contingent army, many sources report, was the prohibition of "camp followers." These were women who followed the troops and acted as concubines. Jeanne's own father had previously accused her of being such a woman after he had a prophetic dream in which he had seen her in the company of soldiers. The idea that she would be leading them rather than following was beyond his understanding. The dream had disturbed him so greatly that he told his sons that he would drown her if such a thing ever came to pass. And if he couldn't do it, they would have to. It was probably for this reason that Jeanne lied to her family when she set out to see Robert de Baudricourt.

The population of Orléans was about 30,000 when the English descended on the walled city. Most of them were safe, at least temporarily, inside its fortified barriers. Because the invaders could not penetrate the walls, which were equipped with 21 mounted cannons, they decided to surround it and wait. Sooner or later, they reasoned, the city would run short of food and other necessities and would become ripe for attack. Throughout this time, the city had endured hails of arrows and other projectiles from the waiting enemy. They had been in this situation for six months when Jeanne arrived.

As expected, Orléans's stores of food and other supplies were dwindling; the hungry and frightened citizens were near despair. While Jeanne was impatient to engage in the battle she believed God had called her to wage, she was also bent on resupplying Orléans. The army entered with relative ease because the English—whose troops were deserting because of lack of support for the campaign from their home-land—had failed to fully encircle the city.

Author Jay Williams reports that Jeanne's arrival in Orléans "threw the city into furor." Citizens took up arms to join the liberation effort, Williams writes. "Their enthusiasm was tumultuous as they clamored for her to lead them out against the English. They had no doubt that she had been sent by God to fulfill the ancient prophecy and free their land." "The citizens had heard of her voices," Williams writes, "[a]nd now she was there, dressed in armor, looking like an aveng-ing angel, the sword of St. Catherine by her side."

But before she rushed into battle, Jeanne said that God demanded that she give the enemy a chance to surrender peacefully. Many of her commanders, feeling outnumbered and under-equipped, did not argue. Others believed that waiting any longer would give the

English time to organize their defenses. But Jeanne insisted. She dictated a letter ordering the English to leave her country.

The English derided her. It wasn't the first time she had tried to warn England in such a fashion. Shortly before she arrived in Orléans, on March 22, 1429, Jeanne had sent a letter to the King of England and the Duke of Bedford. "[D]o right before the King of Heaven," she implored them. She went on:

> Hand over to the Maiden, who is sent by God the King of Heaven, the keys to all the good towns that you have taken and ravaged in France. She has come here on God's behalf to restore the blood royal. She is quite ready to make peace, if you are willing to do right, that is, to leave France, and to make amends for the injuries you have done. . . . And those among you, archers, soldiers, gentlemen, and others who are now besieging the town of Orléans, get you back in God's name into your own country. And if you will not do so, then expect to hear from the Maiden, who will soon encounter you to your very great detriment.
>
> King of England, if you do not do so, I am a captain, and assure you that wherever I find your people in France, I shall fight them and drive them out and shall make them leave, whether they go willingly or not. And if they will not obey, I shall have them put to death. I am sent here by God the King of Heaven to push you out of France. If they will obey, I shall have mercy on them. And do not think that you hold the kingdom of France by the grace of God the King of Heaven, son of St. Mary. For he who will thus hold it is Charles, the true heir, for it is so desired by God, the King of Heaven. . . . I inform you that wherever we find you we will fight you and will make so great a stir there that not for a thousand years has France seen one as great.
>
> . . . And I beg you, if you desire peace, to answer me in the city of Orléans, where we hope to be very shortly. And if you do not do so, you will well remember it by reason of your great misfortune.

Jeanne's powerful words would not move the enemy, however. So, she launched an assault against the

English forces at Orléans. As Jeanne had predicted, she was wounded during battle. During one conflict, she was struck by an arrow. Accounts vary as to whether the wound was in the neck, chest, or shoulder, but most agree that she herself removed the arrow and quickly leaped back onto her horse, leading her troops with renewed inspiration. "Be not afraid!" she cried. "The English will have no more power over you."

There were several battles in the lifting of the siege and several more that followed at outlying villages. However, in the book, *Saint Joan of Arc*, Vita Sackville-West asserts: "The relief of Orléans was not Jeanne's real achievement. Her exploit here has been much exaggerated, and Orléans is forever historically associated with her name. History does always, for some odd reason, give rise to such disproportionate associations; on examination, they seldom prove to be wholly justified; on examination, one usually finds that they stand as the symbol of the wider truth."

In other words, Sackville-West writes, "Jeanne's real achievement was not the relief of Orléans, but the regeneration of the soul of a flagging France." Mary Gordon offers a slightly different, yet somewhat similar perspective. "The English had left Orléans for good without a major battle," she writes, calling the retreat "inexplicable; their forces were greater, and they probably could have prevailed." Jeanne accomplished in a week's time "what well-trained and well-organized captains had not been able to do in six months."

But, "what are we to make of the Battle of Orléans?" Gordon asks. "Certainly it doesn't suggest that she was a great tactician, as none of the important military decisions were made by her." Gordon does not detract from Jeanne's physical stamina and courage, but writes, "she was a presence whose importance and power stemmed not from any traceable action or behavior, but from an atmosphere that preceded and surrounded her. So it was not necessary for her to do one thing rather

than another; it was necessary only that she be there." Gordon concludes this point noting that the French people at that time needed someone "to break through their paralysis. She broke through and handed them victory." In other words, Jeanne's presence was the greatest strength.

Perhaps more important than handing the besieged French people such a victory was the fact that Jeanne had told them that she would before she did it. Where does an illiterate girl from Domrémy get such foresight and confidence, if not from a voice in her head that she claims is God's.

Page from 15th-century manuscript depicting the siege of Orléans. Jeanne's army entered Orleans with relative ease, since the English had not fully encircled the city. The illustration shows the crucial use of cannons in the siege.

The Duke of Burgundy, otherwise known as Philip the Good, (1396-1467) struck a secret agreement with King Charles VII. Philip agreed to a two-week truce while the former strength of Jeanne's army was waning.

4

CROWNING
AND CAPTURE

Jeanne's victories in battle led to another, more important, personal triumph. The new wave of enthusiasm for a united France—coupled with Jeanne's now forceful nature—helped her to persuade Charles the Dauphin to journey to Reims, where he could now be properly crowned as king. It was still no easy task, since the city was deep in territory sympathetic to the Burgundians.

But on July 17, 1429, the dauphin became King Charles VII of France, and the Maid stood near his side in her white suit of armor, draped in a white satin tunic and holding her banner proudly. Jeanne would be asked later why her standard had such a place of honor at the coronation of Charles, and she would answer: "It had borne the burden; it was only *right* that it should have the honor."

The day of the coronation of King Charles VII was a glorious moment for Jeanne. Her experiences on the battlefield must have been both thrilling and terrifying, but they were also no doubt horrifying and bloody. She had seen the worst violence a young girl at that time could have imagined—although she later testified that, despite the weaponry she carried into the fray, she never killed anyone herself. Nevertheless, the day of the coronation was one of pageantry and pomp, not murder and mayhem. It was also the start of a political spiral that would end in her death in less than a year's time. The king she'd led to the crown would later betray her.

Jeanne had now set her sights on liberating Paris, but Charles had other plans. Mostly because of the wild popularity of the Maid of Orléans, the new king had an army larger than his kingdom had seen in some time—or could sustain, for that matter. He had no resources to fund such an army. And an all-out attack on Paris would surely deplete his finances. Charles's hesitation was more than financial, though, as several authors have related. He was also slow to make decisions and preferred to *consider* actions at great length before *committing* to action. This was in stark contrast to Jeanne's headstrong direct approaches. So as she was prodding him to order a march on Paris, Charles was secretly striking political deals with the Duke of Burgundy, signing a two-week truce to negotiate rather than riding the soon-to-wane momentum of Jeanne's military victories.

Jeanne was angered by Charles's actions, but still respected her king. However, she would not be swayed from what she saw as her mission, no matter how unsure the king seemed. And while they weren't making much headway toward Paris, several other Burgundian towns were now surrendering to Charles, including Compiègne, where he stayed while Jeanne's captains waged some half-hearted skirmishes against the defenses of

The beginning of Jeanne's demise took place in front of the gates of the town of Compiègne. It was at this spot where she was seized by the a Burgundian force and received no protection from King Charles VII. After seven months of negotiations, the English bid 10,000 pounds to take her into custody and try her for heresy.

Paris starting on September 8. These minor battles marked the first time Jeanne's forces had been turned back, which began to widen the wedge now forming between her and the confidence she had once inspired in the soldiers. She was once again wounded by an arrow—this time, in the thigh.

Jeanne's army was disbanded on September 22. Lack of funds was cited. Jeanne's king commanded her to abandon the attack on Paris, and she discarded her armor at the cathedral of St. Denis. Authors Regine Pernoud and Marie-Veronique Clin write that "from the days following the coronation of Charles VII at Reims to her capture by a Burgundian force at Compiègne," Jeanne "experienced nearly constant waves of disillusionment. She had made Charles king but was forced to accept the consequences: evasive and suspicious, Charles preferred delay and negotiation to the swift, decisive action to which [Jeanne] was naturally inclined."

The "capture" the authors cite came on May 23, 1430, as Jeanne was retreating from an assignment to quell a minor bandit problem in central France with a small band of mercenaries at her disposal. A Burgundian force caught her just outside of Compiègne's gate. The drawbridge that would have granted her safe passage and refuge inside had been suspiciously raised. Whether it was a mistake or outright betrayal that led to her capture, it has been reported that she fought valiantly, with her back to the city's walls as her only protection. She was pulled off her horse and seized.

For the next seven months, Jeanne was "bid" on as if she were valuable property. The English made the highest offer—10,000 pounds—with Pierre Cauchon, the bishop of Beauvais coordinating the arrangements. She was held captive at several locations and made several unsuccessful attempts to escape before she was finally taken to Rouen for her trial. Not once did King Charles VII offer ransom for France's heroine.

*Pierre Cauchon, Bishop of Beauvais presided over the trial of Jeanne d'Arc in Rouen.
In this illustrated manuscript, we see him condemning Jeanne d'Arc for heresy.*

5

THE TRIAL

After Jeanne the Maid spent months of captivity in the damp dungeons of Rouen, her trial began on February 21, 1431. The chief inquisitor for Jeanne's trial was Pierre Cauchon, Bishop of Beauvais, who had sought refuge in Rouen after Beauvais had expelled the English and the Burgundians nearly three years earlier. Rouen, however, remained sympathetic to the English.

Cauchon had been born about 1371 near Reims, and he studied at the University of Paris. He was licensed in law in 1398. He was elected Bishop of Beauvais on August 21, 1420, on the recommendation of the University of Paris. He served the English party from that time and followed Henry V to Paris. It is documented that he was placed in charge of important missions. He was expelled from Beauvais with the English in August 1429 and fled to Rouen, a place he had already visited many times.

At 8 A.M. on Wednesday, February 21, according to one translation of the records of Jeanne's trial, her first public examination began in the Chapel Royal of the Castle of Rouen. Cauchon reportedly had 42 assessors present. After reading royal letters conveying the surrender and deliverance of the young woman into their hands, Jeanne's request to hear Mass before her trial was discussed by her captors. However, after considering the crimes of which she had been accused and the attire that she was wearing—her boyish garb—they decided to deny her request.

It was recorded on behalf of her inquisitors:

> . . . Then, wishing only to fulfill the duties of our office for the exaltation and preservation of the Catholic Faith, we did first charitably warn and require the said Jeanne, seated in our presence, for the more prompt resolution of the action and the relief of her own conscience, to speak the whole truth upon all questions that should be addressed to her touching the Faith. And we did exhort her to avoid all subterfuges and falsehoods of such a nature as should turn her aside from a sincere and true avowal.

In other words, the judges claimed they asked her to tell the truth in all of her answers, and to do so for the sake of her own soul. However, many scholars have interpreted their words as the first of many attempts to confuse her and trick her into giving the answers they wanted to hear—the answers that would help them to find her guilty of the crimes of which they had accused her.

One of the accusations her inquisitors were formulating was that she was a witch. As a result, the young woman was garbed in her black clothing and chained so that she might not "fly away," as witches were believed to be able to do. Note that no formal charges had actually been made, which helps to explain the ease with which her "conviction" was overturned after her death (in a posthumous nullification trial).

Nonetheless, Cauchon and the inquisitors asked Jeanne to swear with her hand on the holy gospels when they asked her to speak the truth in answering all questions. She replied: "I know not upon what you wish to question me; perhaps you may ask me of things which I ought not to tell you." Cauchon then said, "Swear to speak truth on the things which shall be asked you concerning the Faith, and of which you know."

Jeanne answered:

> Of my father and my mother and of what I did after taking the road to France, willingly will I swear. But of the revelations that have come to me from God, to no one will I speak or reveal them, save only to Charles my King, and to you I will not reveal them, even if it cost me my head. I have received them in visions and by secret counsel, and am forbidden to reveal them.

Perhaps in trying to offer some concession, Jeanne added, "Before eight days are gone, I shall know if I may reveal them to you."

But this only caused great uproar among the inquisitors, and they again warned her to speak the truth, often shouting and interrupting her attempts to answer. Jeanne finally dropped to her knees and swore to speak truth on what she knew in the matter of the faith, but she continued to refuse to communicate to anyone the revelations that had been made to her.

The inquisitors then relented and changed the subject, asking Jeanne to state her name, her surname, her place of birth, the names of her father and mother, the place of her baptism, the names of her godfathers and godmothers and of the priest who baptized her.

> Of my surname I know nothing. I was born in the village of Domrémy, which is really one with the village of Greux. The principal Church is at Greux. My father is called Jacques d'Arc, my mother, Ysabelle. I was baptized in the village of Domrémy. One of my godmothers is called Agnes, another Jeanne and a third, Sibyl. One of my godfathers is called Jean Lingué, another Jean Barrey. I had many other godmothers, or so I have heard from my mother. I was, I believe, baptized by Messier Jean Minet. He still lives, so far as I know. I am, I should say, about nineteen years of age.

"Say your Pater," Cauchon commanded, ordering

the girl to recite the Lord's Prayer. But Jeanne refused because she had been denied the right to confess her sins to a priest.

"Hear me in confession, and I will say it willingly," she replied. They were at an impasse.

Next Jeanne's inquisitors discussed her attempts to escape her imprisonment after Jeanne complained that she had been chained. "You have before, and many times, sought, we are told, to get out of the prison, where you are detained; and it is to keep you, more surely that it has been ordered to put you in irons."

"It is true I wished to escape, and so I wish still. Is not this lawful for all prisoners?" she said, maintaining that escape is the right of any prisoner, if it is possible. "If ever I do escape, no one shall reproach me with having broken or violated my faith, not having given my word to any one, whosoever it may be."

At the end of the first inquisition, a guard was ordered to watch Jeanne in addition to the five English guards that had already been assigned to her. But this additional guard was under orders to permit no one to have dealings with Jeanne without the bishop's order. This was most likely a method of protecting her from her rude and often threatening English captors. The proceeding was adjourned, and Jeanne was ordered to appear before them again the next morning in the Ornament Room, at the end of the Great Hall of the Castle of Rouen.

On the second day of her trial, Jeanne's public examination was held with the bishop and 48 assessors present. The inquisitors had summoned Jean Lemaitre, Deputy of the Chief Inquisitor, to join them. But Lemaitre refused, giving one reason as "for the peace of his own conscience." Nonetheless, he had no objection to the trial continuing without interruption.

Jeanne was brought in and warned again to "swear simply and absolutely to speak the truth on all things," as she had the day before. She answered: "I swore

Photograph of the Castle in Rouen in which Jeanne was imprisoned until her execution. Jeanne's first public examination was held in the Chapel Royal of the castle.

yesterday. That should be enough." Jeanne was told, "Not even a prince, required to swear in a matter of faith, can refuse." "I made oath to you yesterday," she answered, "that should be quite enough for you: you overburden me too much!"

It was then that Maitre Jean Beaupère, a well-known teacher of religious studies, began to question her.

Beaupère: First of all, I exhort you, as you have so sworn, to tell the truth on what I am about to ask you.

Jeanne: You may well ask me some things on which I shall

tell you the truth and some on which I shall not tell it to you. If you were well informed about me, you would wish to have me out of your hands. I have done nothing except by revelation.

Beaupère: How old were you when you left your father's house?

Jeanne: On the subject of my age I cannot vouch.

Beaupère: In your youth, did you learn any trade?

Jeanne: Yes. I learned to spin and to sew. In sewing and spinning, I fear no woman in Rouen. For dread of the Burgundians, I left my father's house and went to the town of Neufchateau in Lorraine, to the house of a woman named La Rousse, where I sojourned about fifteen days. When I was at home with my father, I employed myself with the ordinary cares of the house. I did not go to the fields with the sheep and the other animals.

Jeanne also talked about her confessions, which she made often, and receiving the Holy Sacraments. But when she was asked if she had received the Sacrament of the Eucharist at any time other than at the Easter feast, she replied "*passez outre,*" which means, "pass that by." Jeanne replied "*passez outre*" often during her inquisitions. It was her way of saying that she was not going to answer that question.

Next, Jeanne told her judges: "I was thirteen when I had a voice from God for my help and guidance. The first time that I heard this voice, I was very much frightened. It was midday, in the summer, in my father's garden. I had not fasted the day before. I heard this voice to my right, towards the church."

Uninterrupted, she continued with more specific details: "Rarely do I hear it without it being accompanied also by a light. This light comes from the same side as the voice. Generally it is a great light. Since I came into France, I have often heard this voice."

"But how could you see this light that you speak of, when the light was at the side?" they asked Jeanne.

But Jeanne did not answer that query, choosing instead to go on to something else. "If I were in a wood, I could easily hear the voice that came to me. It seemed to me to come from lips I should reverence. I believe it was sent to me from God. When I heard it for the third time, I recognized that it was the voice of an angel. This voice has always guarded me well, and I have always understood it. It instructed me to be good and to go often to Church. It told me it was necessary for me to come into France."

Jeanne actually was in France, but the interpretation of her reply is that she left her small, outlying village and traveled to Chinon. Nonetheless, her judges listened intently.

"It came to me two or three times a week," she went on. "My father knew nothing of my going. The voice said to me, 'Go into France!' I could stay no longer. It said to me, 'Go, raise the siege which is being made before the City of Orléans. 'Go!' it added, 'to Robert de Baudricourt, Captain of Vaucouleurs. He will furnish you with an escort to accompany you.' And I replied that I was but a poor girl, who knew nothing of riding or fighting. I went to my uncle and said that I wished to stay near him for a time and I remained there for eight days. I said to him, 'I must go to Vaucouleurs.' He took me there."

Jeanne told her inquisitors that when she arrived in Vaucouleurs, she recognized Robert de Baudricourt, although she had never laid eyes on him. She explained that her voice told her how to recognize him. I said to Robert, 'I must go into France!' Twice Robert refused to hear me, and repulsed me. The third time, he received me, and furnished me with men. The voice had told me it would be thus."

She explained that the Duke of Lorraine had then given orders to have her brought to him. "I went there," Jeanne said. "I told him that I wished to go into France. The Duke asked me questions about his health, but I said of that I knew nothing. I spoke to him little of my journey. I told him he was to send his son with me, together with some people to conduct me to France, and that I would pray to God for his health."

The young woman reported that she then returned to Vaucouleurs and from there set out—dressed as a man and armed with a sword given to her by Robert de Baudricourt, "but without other arms."

"I had with me a knight," Jeanne added, referring to Jean de Novelomport, who was also called de Metz. She also listed vaguely Bertrand de Poulengey, Colet de Vienne, the king's messenger, and three servants, and noted that she slept in an abbey when they reached the town of St. Urbain and heard Mass in the principal church when she passed through the towns of Auxerre.

"Who counseled you to take a man's dress?" she was asked. She refused to answer several times. Finally, she admitted: "with that I charge no one."

It is also said that she varied her answer to this question many times. For examples, she said: "Robert de Baudricourt made those who went with me swear to conduct me well and safely, 'Go,' said Robert de Baudricourt to me, 'Go! and let come what may!' I know well that God loves the Duke d'Orléans. I have had more revelations about him than about any man alive, except my king. It was necessary for me to change my woman's garments for a man's dress. My counsel thereon said well. . . . I went without hindrance to the king."

"When I entered the room where he [de Baudricourt] was I recognized him among many others by the counsel of my voice, which revealed him to me," Jeanne told the court. "I told him that I wished to go and make war on the English."

Jeanne said the members of the party she had traveled with "knew well that the voice had been sent me from God. They have seen and known this voice, I am sure of it. My king and many others have also heard and seen the voices that came to me. There is not a day when I do not hear this voice, and I have much need of it. But never have I asked of it any recompense but the salvation of my soul."

At the end of the second day's proceedings, the court adjourned and the next session was set for the coming Saturday, at 8 A.M.

On Saturday, February 24, the third day of Jeanne's third public examination, Cauchon, with 62 assessors present, once again asked Jeanne three times to tell the truth "simply and absolutely on the questions to be addressed to her, without adding any restriction to her oath." She answered: "Give me leave to speak. By my faith! You may well ask me such things as I will not tell you. Perhaps on many of the things you may ask me I shall not tell you truly, especially on those that touch on my revelations, for you may constrain me to say things that I have sworn not to say, then I should be perjured, which you ought not to wish."

To Cauchon, she said, "I tell you, take good heed of what you say, you, who are my judge. You take a great responsibility in thus charging me. I should say that it is enough to have sworn twice . . . all the clergy of Rouen and Paris cannot condemn me if it be not law . . . of my coming I will willingly speak truth, but not of the rest; speak no more of it to me."

She was then again questioned by Beaupère.

Beaupère: How long is it since you have had food and drink?

Jeanne: Since yesterday afternoon.

Beaupère: How long is it since you heard your voices?

Jeanne: I heard them yesterday and to-day. Yesterday I heard them three times, once in the morning, once at Vespers and again when the Ave Maria rang in the evening. I have even heard them oftener than that.

Beaupère: What were you doing yesterday morning when the Voice came to you?

Jeanne: I was asleep. The voice awoke me.

Beaupère: Was it by touching you on the arm?

Jeanne: It awoke me without touching me.

Beaupère: Was it in your room?

Jeanne: Not so far as I know, but in the Castle.

Beaupère: Did you thank it? And did you go on your knees?

Jeanne: I did thank it. I was sitting on the bed, I joined my hands, I implored its help. The voice said to me, "Answer boldly." I asked advice as to how I should answer, begging it to entreat for this the counsel of the Lord. The voice said to me, "Answer boldly. God will help thee." Before I had prayed it to give me counsel, it said to me several words I could not readily understand. After I was awake, it said to me, "Answer boldly."

Jeanne (to the bishop): You say you are my judge. Take care what you are doing, for in truth I am sent by God, and you place yourself in great danger.

Beaupère: Has this voice sometimes varied in its counsel?

Jeanne: I have never found it give two contrary opinions. This night again I heard it say, "Answer boldly."

Then, Jeanne was asked: "The Voice that you say appears to you, does it come directly from an angel, or directly from God, or does it come from one of the saints?"

"The Voice comes to me from God," she said. "And I do not tell you all I know about it. I have far greater fear of doing wrong in saying to you things that would displease it, than I have of answering you."

"Is it displeasing to God to speak the truth?" the judges asked.

"My Voices have entrusted to me certain things to tell to the king, not to you," she replied.

When they asked her, "has your counsel revealed to you that you will escape from prison?" she answered, "I have nothing to tell you about that."

Later in this discourse came one of the most treacherous questions put to Jeanne throughout her trial. It left her in a precarious position. If she answered yes or no, she would have been a heretic.

"Do you know if you are in the grace of God?" they asked. But Jeanne wisely sidestepped the verbal snare in an oft-quoted response:

"If I am not, may God place me there. If I am, may God so keep me. I should be the saddest in all the world if I knew that I were not in the grace of God. But if I were in a state of sin, do you think the voice would come to me?"

Jeanne expressed her disdain for the Burgundians she feared in her village as a child. She recalled that she knew only one back then, and that she would willingly have seen his head cut off "if it pleased God." In an attempt to steer her to another trap, her inquisitors steered her toward discussing old pagan customs that they had learned she may have participated in as a child. It was the best "dirt" their investigators could unearth on her when they were sent to Domrémy before the trial.

"What have you to say about a certain tree which is near to your village?" they asked. "Not far from Domrémy there is a tree that they call 'the Ladies' Tree,'" she replied. She continued:

Others call it "the Fairies' Tree." Nearby, there is a spring where people sick from the fever come to drink, as I have heard, to seek water to restore their health. I have seen them myself come thus, but I do not know if they were healed. I have heard that the sick, once cured, come to this tree to walk about. It is a beautiful tree, a beech. . . . I have sometimes been to play with the young girls, to make garlands for Our Lady of Domrémy. Often I have heard the old folk—they are not of my lineage—say that the fairies haunt this tree. I have also heard one of my Godmothers, named Jeanne, wife of the Marie Aubery of Domrémy, say that she has seen fairies there. Whether it is true, I do not know. As for me, I never saw them that I know of. If I saw them anywhere else, I do not know. I have seen the young girls putting garlands on the branches of this tree, and I myself have sometimes put them there with my companions, sometimes we took these garlands away, sometimes we left them. Ever since I knew that it was necessary for me to come into France, I have given myself up as little as possible to these games and distractions. Since I was grown up, I do not remember to have danced there. I may have danced there formerly, with the other children. I have sung there more than danced.

"Would you like to have a woman's dress?" they asked.

"Give me one, and I will take it and be gone," Jeanne answered. "Otherwise, no. I am content with what I have, since it pleases God that I wear it."

For the fourth public examination of Jeanne the Maid on Tuesday, February 27, the bishop and 54 assessors gathered and repeated their ritual of asking her to swear to tell the truth on everything they asked.

"Willingly will I swear," she answered, "to tell the truth on everything touching the trial, but not all that I know."

Beaupère began to question her again, starting off by asking how she had been since last they spoke. "You can see for yourself how I am," she replied. "I am as well as can be."

He asked if she had fasted and if she had heard the voices since the last session. "Yes, truly, many times," Jeanne answered, adding they told her "nothing that I may repeat to you. . . . I will tell willingly whatever I shall have permission from God to reveal. As to the revelations concerning the King of France, I will not tell them without the permission of my voice."

Jeanne told them that the voices were those of St. Catherine and St. Margaret. "Their faces are adorned with beautiful crowns, very rich and precious. To tell you this I have leave from our Lord. If you doubt this, send to Poitiers, where I was examined before."

Jeanne went on to report that she could tell the voices of the two saintly women apart by the greetings they gave to her. She added: "It is seven years now since they have undertaken to guide me. I know them well because they were named to me. I have also received comfort from Saint Michael."

She related that St. Michael was the first voice that had come to her when she was 13. "I saw him before my eyes, he was not alone, but quite surrounded by the angels of Heaven." Jeanne declined to answer their questions as to what St. Michael was like. "You will

In this engraving, a woman was condemned to death for witchcraft, a relatively common occurrence in the time of Jeanne d'Arc. Witches were the female scapegoats of society. Jeanne's captors also believed she possessed the dark powers of a witch. They chained her to her prison bed for fear she would fly away like a witch.

have no more answer from me. I am not yet free to tell you."

Again the questions turned to her clothing. "Was it God who prescribed to you the dress of a man?" they asked her.

"What concerns this dress is a small thing—less than nothing," she replied. "I did not take it by the advice of any man in the world. I did not take this dress or do anything but by the command of our Lord and of the Angels."

"Did it appear to you that this command to take man's dress was lawful?" they pressed. "All I have done is by Our Lord's command. If I had been told to take some other, I should have done it; because it would have been His command."

"Did you not take this garment by order of Robert de Baudricourt?"

"No."

"Do you think it was well to take a man's dress?" they queried.

"All that I have done by the order of our Lord I think has been well done; I look for good surety and good help in it. I have done nothing in the world but by the order of God."

Jeanne at this point told her accusers that she had been questioned by the clergy at Chinon and Poitiers for three weeks before Charles VII "was willing to believe me." The king also "had a sign of my mission, and the clergy of my party were of opinion that there was nothing but good in my mission."

Jeanne later described her banner and was asked which she cared for most—it, or her sword. "It was I, myself, who bore this banner, when I attacked the enemy to save killing any one, for I have never killed any one."

"What force did your King give you when he set you to work?"

"He gave me 10,000 or 12,000 men. . . . I was

quite certain of raising the siege of Orléans. I had revelation of it. I told this to the King before going there. . . . I had said to them: 'Be fearless, and you will raise the siege.'"

Jeanne then described how she was wounded during the attack on the bridge fortress. "But I had great comfort from St. Catherine, and was cured in less than a fortnight. I did not interrupt for this either my riding or work. I knew quite well that I should be wounded. I had told the King so, but that, notwithstanding, I should go on with my work. This had been revealed to me by the voices of my two Saints—the blessed Catherine and the blessed Margaret."

The young woman boasted slightly of her deeds during the raising of the siege, saying, "It was I who first planted a ladder against the fortress of the Bridge, and it was in raising this ladder that I was wounded in the neck by this cross-bolt."

When Jeanne's fifth public examination was about to begin, she told the Bishop and some 58 assessors, "I am ready."

"As I have already declared to you, to speak the truth on all I know touching this case," she added. "But I know many things which do not touch on this case, and of which there is no need to speak to you. I will speak willingly and in all truth on all that touches this case."

Obviously Jeanne had been giving thought to the opening questions she knew would come. "On what I know touching this Case, I will speak the truth willingly," Jeanne responded. "I will tell you as much as I would to the Pope of Rome, if I were before him."

Later in the inquiry, the judges tried to elicit more details about the appearances of the saints Jeanne claimed visited her, such as what they wore, how they wore their hair, and other characteristics.

"Is their hair long and hanging down?" they asked.

"I know nothing about it," she snapped. "I do not know if they have arms or other members. They speak very well and in very good language; I hear them very well... the voice is beautiful, sweet, and low; it speaks in the French tongue."

"Does not St. Margaret speak English?" an inquisitor asked.

"Why should she speak English, when she is not on the English side?" Jeanne replied.

"In what likeness did St. Michael appear to you?"

"I did not see a crown: I know nothing of his dress."

"Was he naked?" they asked.

"Do you think," Jeanne snapped, "God has not wherewithal to clothe him?"

"Had he hair?"

"Why should it have been cut off?"

Jeanne went on to relate that St. Catherine and St. Margaret "were pleased from time to time to receive my confession, each in turn. If I am in mortal sin, it is without my knowing it."

When she was asked how she summoned her voices, she replied: "Most sweet Lord, in honor of your holy passion, I implore you, if you love me, to instruct me in what I am to say to these churchmen. As regards to my clothes, I fully understand the order by which I accepted them, but I do not know how I am to set them aside. In this may it please you to teach me."

On the sixth and final day of Jeanne's public examination, the bishop and 41 assessors tried once more to trip her up in her oath of truthfulness. "I am ready to swear as I have already done," she said. "I have told you what I know, but to tell you all I know, I would rather that you made me cut my throat. All that I know touching the trial I will tell you willingly."

"Do you think that St. Michael and St. Gabriel have human heads?" they asked her.

"I saw them with my eyes, and I believe it was they as firmly as I believe there is a God," she said.

"Do you think that God made them in the form and fashion that you saw?"

"Yes."

"Do you think that God did from the first create them in this form and fashion?"

"You will have no more at present than what I have answered."

"Do you know by revelation if you will escape?"

"That does not touch on your case. Do you wish me to speak against myself?"

"Have your Voices told you anything?"

"Yes, truly, they have told me that I shall be delivered," she admitted. "But I know neither the day nor the hour. They said to me, 'Be of good courage and keep a cheerful countenance.'"

More questions followed on Jeanne's manner of dress. "Did not your King, your Queen, or some of your party, tell you to take off this man's dress?"

"Yes, truly. And I answered that I would not take it off without leave from God," she said, noting she had been offered a woman's dress, or cloth to make one, and told to wear it, but refused without leave from God. "It was not yet time . . . I did better to obey and serve my sovereign Lord, who is God."

"Did those of your party firmly believe that you were sent from God?"

"I do not know if they believed it," she said. "And in this I refer to their own feeling in this matter. But even though they do not believe, yet am I sent from God."

"Do you not think they have a good belief, if they believe this?" the inquisitors pressed.

"If they think that I am sent from God, they will not be deceived," Jeanne responded. "Many came to see me willingly, they kissed my hands as little as I could help. The poor folk came to me readily, because I never did them any unkindness. On the contrary, I loved to help them."

Questioning later turned to her imprisonment.

"Were you a long time in the Tower at Beaurevoir?"

"About four months," Jeanne replied. "When I

Among the "voices" Jeanne claimed to have heard was the voice of St. Michael the Archangel. Roman Catholics traditionally believe that St. Michael will defend the holy at the Battle of Armageddon —the final battle between the forces of good and evil at the end of time.

knew that the English were come to take me, I was very angry. Nevertheless, my voices forbade me many times to leap. In the end, for fear of the English, I leaped, and commended myself to God and Our Lady. I was wounded."

She added that the voice of St. Catherine told her to "be of good cheer," meaning that she would be healed. Her judges asked her, "What did you say when you had leaped?"

"Some said I was dead," she said. "As soon as the

Burgundians saw I was alive, they reproached me with having leapt."

"Did you not say then, that you would rather die than be in the hands of the English?"

"I said I would rather give up my soul to God than be in the hands of the English."

"Were you not then very angry, to the extent of blaspheming the name of God?"

"Never have I cursed any of the saints," she objected. "And it is not my habit to swear."

When asked if God hated the English, Jeanne said, "Of the love or hate God may have for the English I know nothing, but I know well that they will all be driven out of France, except those who will die here."

The final examination was later concluded and Jeanne was led back to the place where she had been imprisoned in Rouen.

This original 19th-century painting by Delaroche shows Cardinal Winchester interrogating an exhausted Jeanne in her cold prison cell. Jeanne was kept chained to her bed like a dangerous criminal for fear she would attempt another escape. She had previously unsuccessfully attempted several escapes.

6

THE PRIVATE WAR

On March 10, 1431, about three weeks after the last of Jeanne's public examinations—which had failed to yield a shred of proof that she was either a witch or a heretic—Cauchon began interrogating Jeanne in her cell. The questions became more pointed and hostile, and Jeanne's defenses, once bold, were starting to wane from illness, exhaustion, and a lack of sunlight. Nonetheless, the sessions continued, each time growing harder on the Maid. One of the questions that continually recurred was that of her dress. Author Jay Williams states that she told her accusers, "make me a long woman's dress and I shall hear Mass in it, but I beg you to allow me to hear Mass without changing."

The private interrogation ceased on March 18—without Jeanne hearing Mass or changing her attire. On March 27, she was returned to the public arena, where 70 articles outlining her crimes were read to her. For the first time, she was offered the right to have counsel (a lawyer) to speak in her behalf, but she refused, saying: "I have no intention of departing from the counsel of Our Lord."

It reportedly took two days to read the 70 articles of charges lodged against Jeanne. These articles blamed her of virtually everything from engaging in superstition to calling up demons to do her bidding. After she denied the charges, they took her back to her cell and chained her to her cot while the articles against her were condensed to 12.

On Wednesday, May 9th, Jeanne was threatened with torture.

She was brought into the great tower of the castle of Rouen before her judges and others. She was admonished to speak the truth on many different points contained in her trial, which she had denied or to which she had given false replies. The judge read and explained many of the points to Jeanne and told her that if she did not confess to these transgressions truthfully, she would be put to "the torture," the instruments of which had already been shown to her in the tower. There were also torturers present— men standing ready "to restore her to the way and knowledge of truth, and by this means to procure the salvation of her body and soul which by her lying inventions she exposed to such grave perils."

Jeanne answered: "Truly if you were to tear me limb from limb and separate my soul from my body, I would not tell you anything more. And if I did say anything, I should afterwards declare that you had compelled me to say it by force. And if I were condemned and brought to the place of judgment and I saw the torch lit and the executioner ready to kindle the fire, and if I were within the fire, yet I would say nothing else and I would maintain unto death what I have said in this trial!"

The judges said, "Seeing the hardness of her heart and her manner of answering and fearing that the torments of torture would be of little profit to her, we decided to postpone their application until we had received more complete advice on the question."

And so, on Saturday, May 12th, Jeanne's would-be torturers decided not to torture her. Still, Jeanne was weakening.

About two weeks later, on May 24, Jeanne was led to the cemetery behind the Church of St. Ouen outside the city walls, where two wooden platforms had been built. She was decried as a witch and a heretic and read a sentence in which the church officials publicly excommunicated her and told her she would be surrendered over to secular, or civil, authorities (in other words, the English) and burned at the stake. They shaved her head and dressed her in a woman's dress.

Jeanne suddenly agreed to submit to the judgment of her accusers and renounced her visions and voices. This pleased many of the church officials, but greatly angered the English, who wanted her dead.

A document was drafted for Jeanne to sign.

Author John Holland Smith cites the wording of her recantation:

> I, Jeanne the Maid, a miserable sinner, having now realized the sink of error into which I had come and having by the grace of God returned to the Holy Church our Mother, in order that it may be seen I have returned to her not half-heartedly but with good heart and will, do confess that I have grievously sinned by claiming lyingly that I had revelations from God and his angels St. Margaret and St. Catherine and all those my words and acts which are against the church I do repudiate, wishing to remain in union with the church, never leaving it.

Jeanne had reportedly believed that if she recanted, she would be sent to spend the rest of her life in a church prison, where she had wished to be held all along, rather than the English tower, which was filled with sickness and rife with danger. She was led back to her cell in shame.

Although there is much controversy over how and why, it is generally held that on Monday, May 28th,

Jeanne had resumed man's dress when several of her judges came to her prison to observe her state and disposition. She stood in a short mantle, a hood, a doublet, and other garments used by men, which she had previously discarded in favor of woman's dress. Asked when and why she had resumed man's dress, Jeanne answered that she had only recently done this and that she had taken it of her own will under no compulsion. The officials reminded her that she had sworn not to wear man's dress again, but she answered that she never meant to take such an oath.

Jeanne then told her captors that she had originally assumed male costume because it was more lawful and convenient for her to wear such, since she was among men, than to wear woman's dress. She said she had resumed wearing men's clothing after wearing women's clothing because the promises made to her had not been kept. These promises were that they would permit her to go to Mass and receive her Savior and to take off her chains.

When church officials asked Jeanne whether she had not abjured (renounced her oath) and sworn in particular not to resume this male costume, she answered that she would rather die than be in chains. She further said that if she were allowed to go to Mass, if her chains were taken off, and if she were put in a gracious (church) prison and given a woman as companion, she would be good and obey the Church.

In addition to what they could see, Jeanne's judges had also heard that she had not yet severed herself from her illusions and fabricated revelations that she had previously renounced. So they asked her whether she had heard the voices of St. Catherine and St. Margaret since Thursday. She answered yes. When they asked her what the voices had told her, she said that they told her God had sent her word through St. Catherine and St. Margaret of the great pity of this treason by which she consented to abjure and recant in order to save her life and that she had damned herself to save her life. She said that before Thursday they told her what to do and say, which she did. Further her voices told her that when she was on the scaffold before the people she should answer the preacher boldly. They told Jeanne to declare that the preacher was a false preacher, who had accused her of many things she had not done. Jeanne said that if she declared that God had not sent her she would damn herself. For in truth she *was* sent from God. She said that her voices had since told her that she had done a great evil in declaring that what she had done was wrong. She said that what she had declared and recanted on Thursday was "only for fear of the fire."

When Jeanne was told that when she made her abjuration on the scaffold before the judges and the people, she had admitted that she had falsely boasted that her voices were St. Catherine and St. Margaret. She answered that she did not mean to do or say so. She said she did not deny or intend to deny her apparitions, that is, that they were St. Catherine and St. Margaret, and that all that she said was from fear of the fire.

"Through His saints, God informed me of His great sorrow for the treason that I had committed by signing the abjuration. To save my life, I betrayed Him and in so doing I damned myself!" Jeanne said. "My Voices have since told me that I did a great evil in declaring that what I had done was wrong. All that I said and revoked that Thursday, I did for fear of the *fire*!"

After hearing these declarations her judges left her to proceed further according to law. Sources indicate that the words "Responsio Mortifera" were written in the margin of the court notary's paper concerning this statement. This phrase means "fatal answer."

The next day, Tuesday, May 29, the church officials assembled in the chapel of Rouen. With doctors and persons adept in theology and both canon and civil

Photograph of the former Abbey Church of Saint-Ouen in Rouen, France. It was behind this former abbey in the cemetery where Jeanne was condemned and declared a "witch and a heretic." There she was also excommunicated by the Roman Catholic Church. It was decided that her fate would be placed in the hands of the secular authorities (the ruling English). She would pay for her "crimes" with death at the stake.

law in the reverend fathers' presence, Cauchon exhorted Jeanne to return to the way of truth. She refused to acquiesce and said she had nothing further to say. So they pronounced the case concluded and set the sentencing for the following Thursday. Some of Jeanne's judges decided that she should be held as a heretic and given over to the secular justice system, "which should be prayed to act towards her with gentleness." Some declared that Jeanne was "relapsed," and should have the Word of God preached to her. Others felt she should be abandoned to secular authority with no prayer for mercy. Words like "obstinate" and "disobedient" were used in several of the various verdicts.

Jeanne was summoned before the court to hear the sentence of law. They pronounced that a certain woman commonly called Jeanne the Maid was deemed "relapsed into many errors against the faith after a public abjuration of those errors before the face of the Church." They decreed that Jeanne would appear in person before them at 8 A.M. the next day in the Old Market Place of Rouen to hear their declaration of Jeanne as "relapsed, excommunicate, and heretic, with the intimation customary in such cases."

In other words, *Jeanne was sentenced to be burned at the stake.*

In one of the many dramatic representations of Jeanne d'Arc's heroic tale, American thespian Jean Seberg reenacts Jeanne's execution scene in the film St. Jeanne *(based on the play by George Bernard Shaw).*

7

CONDEMNATION AND DEATH

Just before 9 A.M. on Wednesday, May 30, 1431, Jeanne's captors led her to the marketplace before a multitude of people and placed her on the scaffold.

"For her salutary admonition and the edification of the people a solemn sermon was delivered by the distinguished doctor of theology, master Nicolas Midi," states one account, citing his theme as: "Where one member suffers, all the members suffer with it."

In spite of Midi's humanitarian and charitable thought, only one person— a 19-year-old girl—would feel the agony of death by fire that day. When Midi's sermon was over, the judges once more admonished Jeanne to consider the salvation of her soul, reflect upon her misdeeds and truly repent. They begged her to accept the counsel of the clergy, who had tried to teach her things concerning her salvation. Finally it is said that she had, "in her obstinate rashness never truly abandoned her errors and abominable crimes."

The priests and scholars alleged, "by the perjury of God's Holy name and the blasphemy of His saints, she had by such means declared herself incorrigible, a heretic, relapsed in heresy, altogether unworthy of grace and of the communion which, in our earlier sentence, we had mercifully offered her."

They then proceeded with the final sentence, which was recorded as follows:

In the name of the Lord, amen. As often as the poisonous virus of heresy obstinately attaches itself to a member of the Church and transforms him into a limb of Satan, most diligent care must be taken to prevent the foul contagion of this pernicious leprosy from spreading to other parts of the mystic body of Christ. The decrees of the holy Fathers have laid down that hardened heretics must be separated from the midst of the just, rather than permit such pernicious vipers to lodge in the bosom of Our Holy Mother Church, to the great peril of the rest. Therefore, we have declared by a just judgment that you, Jeanne, commonly called The Maid, have fallen into diverse errors and crimes of schism, idolatry, invocation of demons and many other misdeeds. Nevertheless, since the Church never closes her bosom to the wanderer who returns, esteeming that with a pure spirit and unfeigned faith you had cut yourself off from these errors and crimes because on a certain day you renounced them, swore in public, vowed and promised never to return to the said errors or heresy under any influence or in any manner whatever, but rather to remain in the unity of the Catholic Church and the Communion of the Roman pontiff, as is proven at greater length in the formula signed by your own hand. Since after this abjuration of your errors the author of schism and heresy has arisen in your heart, which he has seduced, and since you are fallen again—O, sorrow!— into these errors and crimes as the dog returns to his vomit, as it is sufficiently and manifestly clear from your willing confessions and statements, we have concluded in most celebrated decisions that the denial of your previous inventions and errors was merely verbal. Therefore we declare that you are fallen again into your former errors and under the sentence of excommunication which you originally incurred we decree that you are a relapsed heretic; and by this sentence which we deliver in writing and pronounce from this tribunal, we denounce you as a rotten member, which, so that you shall not infect the other members of Christ, must be cast out of the unity of the Church, cut off from her body, and given over to the secular power: we cast you off, separate and abandon you, praying this same secular power on this side of death and the mutilation of your limbs, to moderate its judgment towards you, and if true signs of repentance appear in you to permit the sacrament of penance to be administered to you.

Jeanne's sentence continued:

You, Jeanne, commonly called The Maid, have been arraigned to account for many pernicious crimes and have been charged in a matter of the faith. And having seen and examined with diligence the course of your trial and all that occurred therein, principally the answers, confessions and affirmations that you made, after having also considered the most notable decision of the masters of the Faculties of Theology and Decrees in the University of Paris, in addition to that of the general assembly of the University, and of the prelates, doctors and men learned in canon and civil law and in theology who were met together in a great multitude in this town of Rouen and elsewhere for the discussion and judgment of your statements, words and deeds, having taken counsel and mature conference with those zealots of the Christian faith, and having seen and weighed all there is to see and weigh in this matter, all that we and any man of judgment and law could and should observe: We, having Christ and the honor of the orthodox faith before our eyes, so that our judgment may seem to emanate from the face of Our Lord, have said and decreed that in the simulation of your revelations and apparitions you have been pernicious, seductive, presumptuous, of light belief, rash, superstitious, a witch, a blasphemer of God and His saints, a despiser of Him in His sacraments, a prevaricator of the divine teaching and the ecclesiastical sanctions, seditious, cruel, apostate, schismatic, erring gravely in our faith, and that by these means you have rashly trespassed against God and the Holy Church.

And it continued:

. . . Therefore, we declare you of right excommunicate and heretic, being stubborn and obstinate in your crimes, excesses and errors; and we pronounce it meet to abandon you and do abandon you to the secular justice as a limb of Satan, infected with the leprosy of heresy, cut off from the Church, in order to prevent the infection of the other members of Christ; praying this same power on this side of death and the mutilation of your limbs to moderate its judgment towards you, and if true signs of penance appear in you to permit the sacrament of penance to be administered to you.

"Alas!" cried Jeanne. "Am I to be so horribly and cruelly treated? Alas! That my body, clean and whole, which has never been corrupted, should this day be consumed and burned to ashes! Ah! I would far rather have my head chopped off seven times over, than to be burned!"

She told her accusers, ". . . had I been in the Church prison, to which I submitted myself, and been guarded by the clergy instead of my enemies, as I was promised, this misfortune would not have come to me! Ah! I appeal to God, the Great Judge, for the great injuries done to me!"

Then, turning to Cauchon, she cried: "Bishop, I die because of you! If you had placed me in the Church's prison and gave me into the hands of competent and suitable Church guardians, this would not have happened. That is why I appeal to God for justice against *you*!"

And Jeanne speaks in her own behalf.

"Everything I have said or done is in the hands of God. I commit myself to Him!" she shouted. "Ha! You take great care to put down in your trial everything that

is against me, but you will not write down anything that is for me! I *am* a good Christian, properly baptized and I will die a good Christian."

"Rouen! Rouen! Must I die here?" Jeanne cried, asking the crowd to "forgive the harm I have done you as I forgive the harm you have done me."

"I ask you priests of God, to please say a Mass for my soul's salvation," she cried. "Please pray for me . . . my voices *did* come from God and everything that I have done was by God's order."

In this 19th century original painting by Patrois one sees Jeanne being led to her execution. It is said that she asked God to forgive her for any harm she had done the people of France as she would forgive the people for the violent death that was imposed upon her.

In her 16th-century manuscript, Diane de Poitiers documents the "rehabilitation" proceedings of Jeanne. This miniature rendering was based on the imagination and recounting by Jeanne's mother, Isabelle Romée. There are conflicting reports as to Jeanne's behavior during her trial. Did she try to outwit her judges? Or was she simply a frightened teenage girl fending for her life?

A paper cap was placed on her head. It read: "Heretic, Relapsed, Apostate, Idolatress."

Then the deadly fire was lit at Jeanne's feet.

"Her end was a slow one," author Mary Gordon notes. "The executioners had been told to keep her a distance from the flames so that the death would be as difficult as possible."

Gordon describes Jeanne's final moments: "She was led up some stairs to the stake to which she was tied. She asked to have a crucifix held in front of her, and an English soldier put together two sticks and gave them to her. Her loyal confessor, Martin Ladvenu, rushed to the church and brought a golden crucifix, which he held in front of her eyes. The fire was lit; soon she was invisible within the flames."

The executioner reported that Jeanne cried out

"Jesus!" at least six times as the flames danced around her. Almost all in attendance cried.

Pernoud and Clin report that Jeanne's ashes were "scattered to the wind." They were thrown into the Seine River "so that no relics could be claimed later."

Nonetheless, rumors flowed after Jeanne's death that her heart had not burned—and that it would not burn. As for her soul, the authors report that one of the assessors at her trial, Jean Alespee, "wept abundantly, according to the witnesses, and said: 'I wish that my soul were where I believe this woman's soul is.'"

A triumphant Jeanne d'Arc looks up to heaven dressed in her armor and short hair. In 1920 she was canonized a saint of the Roman Catholic Church by Pope Benedict XV. Was she a young woman led by a tenacious spiritual dedication or was she ruled by her own delusions or obsession—the world must conclude based on the historical outcomes of her actions.

8

ST. JOAN OF ARC

Jeanne's death gave some momentum to the war effort of the English. After all, the French troops were extremely disheartened. But about a year later, the French began to rally and won more and more battles, often under the leadership of the Maid's former comrades. A treaty was made with Philip of Burgundy in December 1435, and Charles VII's forces took Paris the following year. In 1438, Charles took control of the church in France.

About a decade later, in 1449, the king used that control to ask Pope Nicholas V to authorize a new trial (posthumously) for Jeanne the Maid. Many feel that Charles's gesture was about as humanitarian as was his neglecting to offer a ransom for Jeanne when she was first captured. His sole interest in vindicating Jeanne's name was apparently that it was politically linked to his. In other words, if Jeanne was a heretic and a witch as her killers claimed, what would that make a king who rose to power under her banner and at the tip of her sword?

In his essay, "On the trial of Jeanne D'Arc (translated by Coley

Taylor and Ruth H. Kerr)," Pierre Champion states: "It was a well-ordered trial, a machine of procedure superbly synchronized, put in motion under the highest, most redoubtable authority of that time, the authority of the justice of the Church. . . ." "Never were witnesses and formal evidence received with so much care; no trial of that period—save that of Jean, duc d'Alençon, tried by his peers—was conducted in so impressive and stately a manner," Champion contends, adding, "no trial received such publicity."

"Five authentic copies were drawn up of this great session, circulars were sent to make the conclusions known immediately to the princes of Europe, to ecclesiastics, to cities and it was not wise to speak ill of the Judges of the Maid," he asserts. "This monument of iniquity, this masterpiece of technique has finally borne its fruit. As her judges wished, Jeanne was condemned as a heretic. The English burned her, as they had desired, and they could say, among themselves, that a witch had led Charles, King of France, to the sacrament of Reims."

Because of the formality of the impressive trial of Jeanne d'Arc people didn't speak Jeanne's name in France, except perhaps in Orléans.

Champion writes: "She who had been worshiped in her lifetime, before whom candles had been burned and prayers said, whose ring had been kissed and clothing touched as a sacrament, she who had heard her legend run from one end of Europe to the other, was forgotten . . . authority had spoken."

Yet 18 years later, at the command of Charles VII, efforts were underfoot to undo the travesty of justice toward Jeanne by a nullification trial. The new trial opened in Paris in 1455 and was completed in Rouen the following year. Some 115 witnesses were called forth and interrogated, many of whom were involved in the original condemnation proceedings in 1431.

"It took almost twenty-five years to destroy,"

Champion writes. "Piece by piece—and after endless formalities—this imposing machine that is the 'procès de Condamnation' . . . certainly (by then) many of Jeanne's judges were dead. However, they had lived full of honors and were recipients of benefices."

Champion notes that several among them, when called to make depositions before the Rehabilitation, "lost their memories" and others changed their testimony. Some stated that, "If Jeanne had taken the part of the English instead of that of the French, she would not have been treated in such a way."

On numerous grounds, the condemnation of the Maid was declared to have been procedurally flawed. The trial was ordered nullified—which did Jeanne little good. Nonetheless, on a Sunday in January 1456, all who had known her were invited to Domrémy's village square to give testimony and recount their memories of her. This loving testimony was very different from the one that had sentenced Jeanne to a fiery death. From this testimony came much of what is known about Jeanne's early life today.

Champion reported that Jacques d'Arc had "opposed with all his power the mission of his daughter, whom he wished to marry off." Nonetheless, "he went to Reims for the coronation of the king, and the king and the municipality defrayed his expenses and gave him a horse for his return to Domrémy." He died, it is said, of sorrow over his daughter's execution. Isabelle d'Arc left Domrémy after her husband's death and eventually settled at Orléans. It has been said that Jeanne had also wanted to live in Orléans and had taken a long lease on a house there near St. Catherine's Church. On November 28, 1458, Isabelle, then about 60 years old, died.

Missing from these proceedings was Pierre Cauchon. Historians report that he died suddenly while his beard was being trimmed at St.-Cande, on December 18, 1442—more than a decade before the nullification trial.

It was noted that during her trial, Jeanne had warned the bishop, saying: "You say that you are my judge. I do not know if you are! But I tell you that you must take good care not to judge me wrongly, because you will put yourself in great *danger*. I warn you, so that if God punishes you for it, I would have done my duty by telling you!" Mysterious fates, including leprosy, reportedly befell several of her other judges besides Cauchon.

But Jeanne's life was not about revenge. Granted, it's not a happy tale. But it has inspired people for nearly 600 years. Indeed, the Catholic Church canonized Joan of Arc in 1920. In other words, after lengthy deliberations, the church determined that Jeanne had led an exemplary life and met all the criteria to be called a saint. She is now, as for the past 80 plus years, St. Joan of Arc.

Jeanne has also been the subject of countless studies, books, plays, and films over the past five centuries, and there are no signs of her legend slowing. American satirist Mark Twain penned two serious works on the French heroine. Another popular version of her story—this time in a theatrical setting—was George Bernard Shaw's stage play, "Saint Joan" produced in 1923 and wasting little time in capitalizing on her canonization. But Pernoud and Clin report that plays centered around the maid were staged in Orléans as early as 1435—only four years after her death and nearly two decades before France was united and her condemnation trial was nullified.

While Jeanne's story appeared onscreen as early as 1898, her life was portrayed in the film version, "La Passion de Jeanne d'Arc," which was released in 1928, directed by Carl Dreyer and starring Renée (also known as Maria) Falconetti. Actress Ingrid Bergman played the heroine in the 1948 film, "Joan of Arc."

As recently as 1999, two major films were released with Joan of Arc as heroine. One, simply called *Joan of Arc*, starred Leelee Sobieski; the other, which starred Milla Jovovich, was, *The Messenger: The Story of Joan of Arc*.

But just what was Jeanne's message?

This has been interpreted in thousands of ways—many in some state of agreement, while many more remain mired in conflict and contradiction. Indeed, as author Mary Gordon reports, "there are over 20,000 books about Joan of Arc in the Bibliotheque Nationale in Paris. This figure suggests the impossibility of reading even a substantial portion of what has been written about her."

Among so many works, we can find multiple theories and much evidence to either support or refute the facts we now have about Joan. Some say her military prowess was legendary, while others claim she paraded on a horse in armor while others mapped out mediocre strategies. Some claim she retained her virginity, while others argue that it would have been virtually impossible in her captivity. Some authors contend she was something of a showman during her trial, confounding her captors with her brilliant answers and seemingly enjoying the performance, while others portray her as terrified and praying to her voices for counsel in each response.

We have no way to determine who is right. The best we can hope for is to reach our own conclusions by thoroughly examining the information we have. Was Jeanne just a headstrong girl who got caught up in the swirl of events in her homeland and placed herself in a position to affect those events? Was she so strongly driven by a desire to unite her country that she willingly sacrificed herself? How could she have believed she could survive in a corrupt government? Was Jeanne truly called by God?

Perhaps it is best to decide for ourselves what the Maid was like, what she stood for and what those qualities mean to us. Maybe we can listen to whatever "voices" guide our own lives. This seems to be just what a 19-year-old girl from Domrémy, France, named Jeanne d'Arc did.

CHRONOLOGY

1412	Joan was born at Domrémy on January 6
1415	Henry V invades France
1422	Henry V and Charles VI die; crown dispute between Henry VI and Charles VII
1424	Jeanne first hears voices in mid-summer
1428	Jeanne goes to Vaucouleurs to see Robert de Baudricourt in May; in July she takes refuge at Neufchateau; Domrémy is raided; the English begin the siege at Orléans
1429	Jeanne returns to Vaucouleurs; she arrives in Chinon in March and is granted an audience with Charles the Dauphin. Jeanne is examined by theologians at Poitiers and dictates her first letter to the English; in April she arrives outside Orléans and the siege is raised in May. Jeanne is in Reims for the coronation of King Charles VII; Charles signs a truce with Burgundy. She is wounded in an attack on Paris in September; three months later her family is given a coat of arms and the surname "du Lys"
1430	Jeanne is captured at Compiègne on May 23; she is held prisoner at Beaurevoir and delivered to the English in November
1431	Custody of Jeanne is transferred to Bishop Cauchon; the Trial of Condemnation begins; Jeanne is admonished to recant. In May, the University of Paris' condemnation is read and the trial concludes; Jeanne recants and is sentenced to life in prison but withdraws her recantation and accepts the death sentence four days later. She is burned at the stake on May 30
1455–56	The "Trial of Rehabilitation" is reopened in Paris; the original verdict is thrown out and Jeanne is declared innocent
1904	Pope Pius X confers the title of "Venerable" on Joan of Arc
1920	Pope Benedict XV canonizes Joan of Arc on May 16

Banfield, Susan. *Joan of Arc*. New York: Chelsea House Publishers, 1988.

Gies, Frances. *Joan of Arc: The Legend and the Reality*. New York: Harper & Row Publishers, 1981.

Gordon, Mary. *Joan of Arc*. Middlesex, U.K.: Penguin Books Ltd., 2000.

Lace, William W. *The Hundred Years' War*. San Diego: Lucent Books. 1994.

Paine, Albert Bigelow. *The Girl in the White Armor: The True Story of Joan of Arc*. New York: Macmillan, 1967.

Pernoud, Regine, and Clin, Marie-Veronique. *Joan of Arc: Her Story*. New York: St. Martin's Press, 1999.

Sackville-West, Vita. *Saint Joan of Arc*. London: The Folio Society, 1995.

Smith, John Holland. *Joan of Arc*. New York: Scribner's, 1973.

Twain, Mark. *Personal Recollections of Joan of Arc*. New York: Harper & Row Publishers, 1924.

Warner, Marina. *Joan of Arc: The Image of Female Heroism*. New York: Alfred A. Knopf, 1981.

Williams, Jay. *Joan of Arc*. New York: American Heritage, 1963.

INDEX

INDEX

PICTURE CREDITS

Dwayne E. Pickels has been a general assignment news reporter with the *Tribune-Review* in Greensburg, Pennsylvania, since 1991. He is a graduate of the University of Pittsburgh, where he cofounded and edited the literary magazine *Pendulum*. Dwayne won a Pennsylvania Newspaper Publishers' Association (PNPA) Keystone Press Award in 1992. In 1997, he authored four volumes in the Chelsea House series *Looking into the Past: People, Places and Customs*. He has also written a volume on psychological testing and a biography of Shania Twain. He currently resides in Scottdale, Pennsylvania, with his wife, Mary, and their daughter, Kaidia Leigh. In his free time, he engages in literary pursuits and enjoys outdoor excursions, including bird watching, hiking, photography, cooking and target shooting, along with futile attempts at fishing.

Matina S. Horner was president of Radcliffe College and associate professor of psychology and social relations at Harvard University. She is best known for her studies of women's motivation, achievement, and personality development. Dr. Horner has served on several national boards and advisory councils, including those of the National Science Foundation, Time Inc., and the Women's Research and Education Institute. She earned her B.A. from Bryn Mawr College and her Ph.D. from the University of Michigan, and holds honorary degrees from many colleges and universities, including Mount Holyoke, Smith, Tufts, and the University of Pennsylvania.